A Soul's Journey

Journey

Part- 1

Red Jordan Arobateau

A Soul's Journey–1.
Copyright © 2014, by Red Jordan Arobateau
All rights reserved.

Journal #25 in the Journey Series

Any resemblance to any person living or dead is purely coincidental.

All un-attributed quotes are from the Prophet Red Jordan Arobateau.

Published by RED JORDAN PRESS
Redjordanarobateau.com
USA

Oh, here is the paper of NOTES from the LGBTQ ceremony Milestones toward Marriage Equality @ the cathedral, step by step thru the years up to our current freedom; –so we had to go thru all this! ARURRGH!

1964 Interfaith council on religion and the homosexual is founded in San Francisco

1977 1st openly lesbian priest, is ordained in the Episcopal church

1996 US president signs the Defense Of Marriage Act (DOMA) into law, banning federal government from recognizing same-sex unions

1998 Anglican bishops declare homosexuality is incompatible with scripture

1999 California passes domestic partnerships

2004 Mayor of san Francisco orders city hall to issue marriage license to same sex couples

2004 California supreme court orders San Francesco to stop issuing marriage licenses to same-sex couples and invalidates all same-sex marriages issued that year

2005 California is first state legislature to pass bill legalizing same-sex marriage then governor Arnold Schwarzengger vetoes the bill

2008 California a supreme court rules in favor of same-sex marriage; same sex marriages resume

2008 California voters approve proposition 8 amending the state constitution to exclude same-sex couples from marriage

2009 California Supreme Court upholds proposition 8, same sex marriages stop; marriages from June thru November 2008 remain valid

2010 US District Court declares proposition 8 unconstitutional; the decision is stayed pending appeal

2011 US Ninth Circuit of Appeals upholds ruling that proposition 8 is unconstitutional; decision stayed until US Supreme Court can rule proposition 8 is still in effect; no new same-sex marriages

2012 Supreme Court dismisses ruling making permanent the early ruling that proposition 8 is unconstitutional. They also strike down the section of DOMA which defines marriage solely as between a man and a woman

2012 Ninth Circuit lifts its stay of the district courts ruling; same-sex marriage resume in California.

But across the ocean on the continent of Africa, is the complete opposite. Nigeria presents legislation passing a huge homo-murderous bill—life imprisonment for all homosexuals; all those citizens who know of a homosexual must turn them into the police. This has been widely condemned through the world.

Tuesday, February 18
Went by Meridian Art Gallery—left biz card only.

They did not want anything else—*prefer if you send us an e-mail w/attachment of your works, & bio.*

So now, the OM had gone by 2-cross outs on his short list of art galleries to show his Fine Arts work.

TV program showed one of the Wythe sisters—daughter to Andrew Wythe—famous painter. All the family painted. This sister painted only 4 paintings per year. Today they sell from around $15,000. Some children never leave home, they stay in the protective shelter of their birth family house—if they are fortunate enough to maintain this. And she was one.

Found a can of beef stew and 25¢.

On wei to Coyote.

Approached Coyote; customary cocooned homeless lays on sidewalk; being its nearby a large thoroughfare—Polk Street—and thus more grime, less police complaints.

Am @ Coyote there's hardly any sun thru the fog—simply bright light.

Now sun has grown brighter.

See the butch dike prostitute walk past, gaunt. Wearing men's clothes. She is mean. A soul unrecognized.

Nuts enough to be housed I believe, on SSI…

You must never regret how things would have played out—if you had arrived a minute later, or someone else had left a while before—for its God's will.

Might not have seen me, but now, Junior saw the Singing Man & started coming over, and sure enough there I was also.

Never seen Junior look so bad—so messed up on drugs, argumentative, and almost mean.

I was invigorated by social contact.

Wait for Junior to return, watching his backpack—he carrying his usual walking stick.

Junior is bald headed.

Didn't you know I was a jailhouse barber?

Well God plays a hard, fast game.

They were the worst of what they are because it is their <u>power</u>. Every other social grace deserted them but their main power—being stubborn, or being liars, or being ego-driven. As they fail in life, every other facet of their personality becomes this one power they have—which destroys them.

Be what God would have us be instead—The Creator has set in place a good defining line.

Wild, babbling, filthy hands, dirty face; high on Meth.

The creature people.

Aurrgghh! Hard headed.

This stupid Junior; having a difficult time w/him—it is the chemicals he's ingested.

Saw him one night on acid, says one of the baristas, sarcastically— this hard-working barista, he was once a street kid, but he's bettered himself.

I tell Junior not to take his garbage into the café—but he stands there stupidly; high on meth and argumentative. *Don't talk to me like I was a dog.*

Felt very shaky after this encounter

PM

We GLBT of an older generation can be very derogatory of ourselves—*that stomping dyke, that fairy queen*—transsexuals can be the hardest on themselves, the Male To Female kind. These modern days, pride has come into being, and many of the new, middleclass variety of us Queers have self pride, are positive, and stand in their position—never shirking from it by being self-depreciating. This bitter cynicism, this self-censorship; it is of an age. I recall the 1950's and before in the racial community: Blax folks would ridicule their own hair—fingering a strand of it wooly, kinky, calling it: *yo' lucky yo' hair ain't trash like mines.*

> The Golden Shower bums spent their crisp $10 and $20 here, and the toefreak—who had a real Doctors degree, exchanged pharmaceutical scripts for the pleasure of sucking the nasty toes of the most hideous skid row bums. Flicked his tongue cleaning jam from between their knurled yellow-nail toes. He was black, and he only sucked white male toes; worshiping male feet; groveling, subservient to their feet until he was done. No sex. Just a silent, controlled climax staining his pants front. Duke had been with him & Freddy too. A line of men, victims of skid row peeled off their filthy shoes & sox. To allow him to salivate over their feet. Each received a prescription for Amphetamine, or Codeine—30 tablets. They had to buy it themselves.
>
> Hags were scattered among the drinking men; their grey hair long, disheveled. Wrinkled skin. Beer mugs held in withered hands. – Some had once been wives. Some were whores. Basically they had been dumb. After the first lies they'd told were mastered to perfection, and their art of swiping change off the bar, or wallets from a sucker—for all their game of those past golden years, here they were down at the bottom of the nightmare sea with problems & nothing to call their own. They had lived a fast, dumb life.
> --LUCKY & MICKEY

6

Ukraine. Downtown Kiev is in fire! Middle-aged women are hacking up the pavement w/pick axes providing stones to throw @ police. People build barricades w/stone and wood ripped from government buildings. Tires in large piles are set on fire! They do not want to return to the Russian regime!

Oh—a while ago w/a wiser head then my own, speaking of the African battles which go back, far back, way beyond when white men first set foot on the land—the tribal battles— and I mentioned how the same thing could happen here if conditions were right, and we discussed the idea of retribution:

> Revenge.
>
> No! Because it doesn't work, that's why!

I'll tell you honestly I don't think people really understand what's happening to them in this life—all its twists & turns. Me & Jasmin for instance, am still bewildered, —after 12 years.

Wednesday, February 19
Protests by renters & the poor have been mounting and are reaching critical mass in this city— they all know, now, —those yuppies, they have all heard by now... they know we hate them.

> They're buying the city.
> --L. Therapist

The younger tek industry—the city is being arranged for them.

Believe.

Am @ Coyote. Sun bright, but its windy.

Well yes—am glad I came out here to SF, 1967, California Dreamen', thank God had:

> Wrote books (102 +)
> Met Jasmin & had 16.5 year relationship/marriage
> Transitioned my gender
> Found God

7

To drag myself awake from sameness, from the average—or from drunkenness, to become an artist, to actually achieve art—was a major hurdle broken. It ain't easy to take risks. To step out. To sacrifice comforts. To <u>awake.</u>

The one extraordinary thing you've done w/your life.

The high hell holy voice of a gay man goes past.

Hag, used/abused so bad; in bluejeans w/no belt which slide half way off her; stoops down, picks thru garbage among the table & chair legs—wildly pawing trash out into middle of sidewalk, her white round bare ass poking out in air. Latina walks by w/scarf around her neck, pulls it up so it becomes a veil—to cover the side of her face facing the view, so as not to see: *Aww nah! Ahh nah! Pull you pants up, dey so low!*

Next, the older woman who gave me/us sort of a hard time @ BABYLON FALLING our bookstore—She was one of those who created Rent Control acts in times gone by. (1947, revised 1979.) What new battles have we now?

A human dog barer goes by, carrying dog in her arms; dog sits upright, its furry tan tummy warmed by sunlight—blissfull expression on its doggy face.

The OM sat in bright sun—listened to beautiful music issuing forth from the Café, as stream of people walked past, some w/dogs; he fantasized many movies he would make proclaiming the Most High & the *truth, & justice!*

Chill wind begins to blow—

If you are born w/a talent & you are early recognized for it by adults & given some place, honor or credit doing it in your youth— your feet first have been placed upon The Path. —You may well feel the urge to follow it for a lifetime. –Then you say: *thank You God, for employing me.*

Your Calling.

In the next block as he sat, resting a moment on a fire hydrant, he saw Junior; recognized him by his bald head. He was walking w/out his acustomary walking stick. He did not seem high: *Come on, I'll buy you a donut.* The bald head youth mumbled, after a moments hesitation, his eyes sparkling bright.

The young man was constrained. He would recall he'd done wrong the last time they'd met & hesitate talking to the OM, & was going to walk by.

Weather is now cold. OM walked quickly, on his wei to Grant Writing Center to crank out biz.

Transsexual—it's a very difficult journey. So difficult that some don't take it. Some don't make it.

PM
M'Gawd, have yuh heard this? One of the Social Networking media outfits has purchased anther start-up firm for 16 billion dollars!! Yes, Billions!

The battle of the moguls takes place on the chessboard of life, and any in their path are knocked off-course—the sweeping diagonal thrust of the angry queen, machinations of the clever bishop, strange movements of those knighted, the trompling of the common herd of pawns; you are rushing to survive their tidal wave; Watch Out!

Red was in a merry mood when he got home—was part of this having seen Junior, and he looked not-high; normal, and they'd exchanged a sort-of hello?

> Our reporter is here; he's seen 3 protesters shot dead by machine gun fire, by the guards—in the 1st hour.
> --French TV, Kiev, Ukraine

> ***

> Lust for a transwoman's stiff rod! "Ohhh!" She speaks again, as we both gaze down at her lovely penis--like a little girl discovering a

9

big secret; "Ohhhh look Daddy!" They both breathe faster, excited. Perspiration beads their skin. Transman puts his small strong hand on her phallus; cups it, strokes down to her balls; a neat package. Will he allow her to service his hot cunt? Slide her thick penis into him and move, ecstatically, moaning and making rapid fire little thrusts? "I've served you Daddy, now, can I give us both pleasure?" Cher inquires in her tiny, high, little-girl voice which is a caricature; Cher has finally mastered the art of speaking in a high voice after 3 -years transition, her pretty powdered bull neck having slenderized housing her now trained thick male vocal cords and she loved to use it! A pink tongue tip flecked over broad red painted lips smooth and blinks her big wide eyes with long curled lashes & blue eyeshadow. "Please Daddy! It would be so much fun! As he feels her dong, squeezes it while drinking in the sight of its helmet shaped dickhead & thick shaft, now quivering straight as an arrow out of her bare, shaved pubis mound; face still wet from having swallowed Transman's cock-cunt juice: "Let me enjoy you in another way..." She winks, suggestively. Bats her eyelashes flirtatiously; her wares standing bone hard there on display. "Oh Daddy My Little Man, please let me go in! I'll do it for the both of US! I'd like nothing better then to stick my long pussy in there...' She giggled & pointed to Red's pubic area with a painted tip finger. The perversion of it aroused flames of Eros in him, maintaining a strong rush of libido; and desire caused him to stroke her long phallus slowly, up from its base, rising to its tip, passing his thumb over her throbbing dickhead, then going back down, squeezing her erotic meat. "DADDY PLEASE!" Cher stomped one foot in its high-heeled pump --a grand size 16--impatiently.

"PLEASE LET ME! It won't hurt! I promise! I know what I'm doing... Yes I do!" And wiggled away--to arms length, performing a sensuous dance half naked, tall, brown, on top of her golden pumps, slender hips swaying, midriff sucks air in/out, her voluminous breasts jugging to her instantaneous rhythm--broad face smiling like a party doll. Her big dong bouncing; now she holds it in the yellow-brown palm of her open hand, offertory---like a gift:
....."UHHHMMMMMMMMMMM... Transman leans back against the dim, shadowy wall, acquiescing. "I know how wet you are from all my hard work..." She murmurs, her large face grows near, she holds her female phallus in one big perfumed hand, and begins to

stroke its tip into Transman's wet, vulva which is ready, puffed up with lust, expectant to receive... She bends over him; they both exude scent of perfume, pheromones and sweat... Cher stands wide legged, makes herself shorter, so she can enter him easier. Soon her virile rod's gliding in & out of his hot chamber excitedly; her ass swishing up/down. "OH SO GOOD! SO GOOD!" Her legs spread wide, arched feet on golden pumps, nyloned legs shimmering; her hips thrust in/out; runs the tip of her dick over his clit cock, stimulating it over & over, then slowly pushes in, then pulls almost all the way out, then in, deep, deeper.. "OH HIS PUSSY IS SO JUICY!" She moans, thrusting vigorously. "OH HIS PUSSY IS SO WET! "Ummmmmm..." Transman's head tips back, ecstatic. "UH.. I LIKE THE WAY PUSSY FEELS! UHHHH UHHH!" Declares the tall girl. "Uh... I like the way this cock feels uhmmmmmmmm." Transman grunts, his yellow hips thrust forward to meet her driving phallus in tempo. In addition, she likes nothing better then to stick her hard dick into some soft wet pussy.
--STREET OF DREAMS

Thursday, February 20
Coyote. No OGM's here—occasional sightings—the sun is here however—a delight & me w/some cash! Been seated w/my coffee many days now—become a paying customer. It is sad when all you have to look forward to is a funeral (Memorial Service) @ Grace—it will be fun—gathered together in My Name.—The elephants have funerals as you know—all the big grey mammals gather together carrying a leafy branch in their trunks and place it on top of their fallen friend. Nature has memories. Even the dolphins have watery rituals upon death—baring the dead dolphin up w/their snouts up to the surface.

Polk Street; elegantly attired dog trots past—older Asian man on the other end of the leash; its red suit includes pantaloons which cover its hind legs to the feet.

Steppen' music plays; blax music. Step beat beat step step.

Step on time.

He tried making a few phone calls; numbers he knew.

11

To serve God you have to be in agreement—not simply to say *I agree*—but to be in a state within yourself of agreement. To be in a state of agreement w/the Lord/ess.

Work on it Red Jordan.

This is the path many miracles are accomplished thru human hands (from God's power) by being a prayer already prepared w/in oneself.

Woman don't say half the stuff the could---fear of male violence & harassment.

So he sat there biding his time—until 4-oclock—like a Madame Defarge knitting together his powerful words into infamous NOTES put together & found in JOURNEY Journals the world now knows. These words are for you, and you, and you....

Each word is an invitation from the Most High—who by convoluted ways reaches out to us, just as Julian of Norwich (born 1342, England in the catholic church of St Julian, in Norwich) – in her hermitage; cemented in, brick by brick against a wall of this church; created songs, paintings, and writings, done within the most strict confinement first also prepared the way; as so did the prophets in their writings & scriptures, verses, passages, prepare the way—since time immemorial—forging God's pathway into human life (& the elephant tribes) and those before us.

Do you know Google filled a whole office building over on Alabama street? Simple people, poor, but decent clothes go past—speaking w/new apprehension into their cell phones, unhappy, astounded, using this modern media themselves, but horrified @ the human cost, the toll in peoples lives it is making—like a digital nuclear bomb dropped on the poorest in Amerikkkan cities.

It is absolutely vital the people know about the existence of the God/ess not for the sake of getting to heaven—but for existence on this cruel earth—they won't be able to make it alone. Their lives will be decimated by twists of random fate. By unholy premeditation of other humanbeings for their own advantage. I know for a fact this world is supremely cruel.

The sun is so beautiful, blazing down from sky set there faithfully day-by-day ever since our eternity—I thank God/ess for this.

So here the miasma passes, the flotsam/jetsam forth/back. La Strada.

OM sat there @ a perfect angle so bright yellow sun shone directly past the tree/bush upon him—but shadow had overtaken the table next to his where sat the kindly cute K, gay bartender from Mark's Place down several blocks, w/friend.

The gold cauldrons were totally gone to disrepair—green leaves sprouted gangly into weeds, each cauldron w/a tree in it; no flowers remained.

Sun blazed high in sky, blue/white clouds blazing bright, fierce.

The sun majestic sets on a pale blue sky-- so high up.

Now screaming is heard, angry, male, a bicyclist hollers @ a driver in a new, compact car who pushes him out of the road; YEAH! YUH GO ON TAKE YOUR RIGHT OF WAY!"

The OM sat writing grimly seated wide-legged in the sunbeam.

A curious onlooker might ask him: *what are you doing?*

He could reply—*making a million dollars—writing a million dollar book!*

I'm walking on sunshine!

I'm feelen' good—so the purpose is to encourage one another—to keep on the road!

The sour smell of the recycler beer sacks & metal cans clanking out here. CLANK, CLANK!

He was nearly home.

Why bother to stay alive? The Malaysian has asked me this a dozen times now, and I have heard it before—from many—depressed souls, challenged souls, especially among youth, and from the black/brown community—heard it done, tho not said in so many words, as they take on the mantle of narcotics/alcohol, to shield them from harm, to mask their existence passing thru this world.

For some of us life might be bearable enough with many joys & delights sprinkled along the way.

PM
Kiev—protesters have taken 57 policemen hostage! Hurrah! Yeah for Freedom! Death toll has mounted, w/police snipers firing live rounds into the crowds of protesters—young people, and middle-aged women & men!

78-deaths so far—in the last 2 days.

This is going to turn into a civil war if something is not done immediately to patch things up!

Worst violence since the end of the Soviet Union.

Almost finished working for the night—am going to lay down in my <u>bed!</u>

A bed well made Red Jordan.

HA HA HA HA HA! Vatican bank exposed money laundering Mafia money! –For half a century! HA HA HA HA!

Friday, February 21
Jasmin PU OM on wei; 16h/Capp street—right off of Mission, drug capitol of California—site of the old Victoria Theater were we did our command performance for 6 wonderful weeks. –To Native American

14

Dental clinic. Jasmin was afraid to park directly outside for there was a deranged-appearing blax street man—agitatedly pacing around a parking meter w/a wild look on his face; she had good reason. Transman walked back past him to go in:

> How can you capture a bootie—if you don't attack?

Inside the clinic received my crown from the nice Vietnamese Dr:

> Here isn't this a lovely crown? A crown for a king!

She is full of encouraging words—which makes our time go easier.

They mentioned my fat tongue:

> Mr. Red you have a fat tongue. We have to push your tongue out of the way to polish the crown. Even Doctor XX says you have a fat tongue! All the doctors have mentioned it! The only reason we talk about your fat tongue is that it gets in our way!

Beautiful hot day out!

As said, dis heah be the barrio. Po'. People on lowest level of human existence; sag mouth, no teeth, hair bad.

The trank has wiped me out, calmed me down.

The sun is towering in warmth.

Brief fun @ Coyote w/3 OGM & 1 youngish one. A birthday lad— just turning 86! Sex drive still churning out, but can't get it up. Oh well. He looks very well for his age. Next in line a dapper gent—76; then there's me @ 70—almost, then two spring chickens in their 50's.

Coyote. A switch walks bi—who has his dick in both de girls & de boyz.

On corner of California/Larkin a policeman is moving traffic along, STAY ON THE SIDEWALK! STAY ON THE SIDEWALK! 15, 20, police squad cars, — flashing red, yellow, lights; then come the big vans full of Homeland Security officers; now a crowd has gathered on the sidewalk—TM was so glad he'd crossed the street a block behind, now he was free to walk; and then more black limonene and sleek elegant vans drive by full of men & a few women in suit-uniforms of Homeland Security team; a dignitary is in town.

Overhead in the sky a helicopter hovers keeping an eye on it all.

The Dali Lama is visiting San Francisco.

Ho's; went in and got a fruit health bar, & fed the pigeon. Talked briefly. Crosier—the Bishops staff.

PM
Nada.

Saturday, February 22
Funeral service; God damn. Bishop addresses us. Heard it now, tho have heard it thousands of times before here:

> Those who don't want to take the Blood but simply want a blessing come forth and cross your arms.

I listen to this for 7 years; done this gesture—but to me it means I want to take the Blood! Not just a blessing! I want the Blood of Christ! Its just that as an alcoholic I simply cannot take one single drink of liquor! So what's the point of this? –Making this folding of the arms over the chest, as if in denial!

After the funeral went to reception w/nice food.

Here are the well-off, the rich even.

Food, plenty of food on several tables, yet I hear some say: *lets go to lunch @ Nob Hill Cafe*. This really shows they have cash.

Some are dark—very dark.

No hellos. Overheard many: *how are you my dear,* or *hello there*, or *oh how are you!* No hellos for him—realized as had many times before @ such events, when he should be having a great time—

16

w/food aplenty & good coffee catered by Peets coffee company—that he wasn't exactly having bang-up great time, because he wasn't talking to anyone! And he had no friends, nor cronies w/him.

No hellos for him—but—a brief grunt from a pervert in the men's room.

Transition has many meanings.

It is a difficult time, intern to doctor. From student clergy to ordained deacon. From deacon to priest.

From female to male.

PM
Had fun w/brother Baz, who told me:

> Your aim here is to stay strong. You are surrounded by these rich people. You have to remain you, and be strong in you!
>
> ***
>
> As it stands, the president has been taken out of office; elections are slated to be held shortly, and all police have been w/drawn from the streets. People are looking @ Ukraine as what they call a revolution.
> -French TV

Sunday, February 23
The sun seemed huge descending in the pale white tinge sky. Yellow holds strong for awhile inside the diameter in the Western sky @ full day—then, still later, somewhat thru the mists. Grey white fog. SF fog

Grace.

Foghorn toots out in the bay.

Streamers which hang from the rafters some 8 stories above, blue/red streamed magnificently down; the round sparkling Rosetta stained glass window high up in the cathedral front wall; which is sparkling like a jewel. —The alleluias had begun. He was there—many singers from the men/lesbian choirs —his kind of people— all devout & in service of the Most High; sopranos echoed *alleluia* brilliantly.

He missed Chinese A but it was necessary. –Their separation; rather, her retreat into isolation.

The alleluias soared magnificently & w/power.

A work of High Christianity—service to God.

He lit his candle.

The fog was thick sky over 3 of the Wealthiest hotels on earth—in empire— the Huntington, Fairmont, Mark Hopkins—where Washington DC Politico dignitaries, presidents, presidents wives, visit, debarking from their motorcades.

The red white & blue American flags flew, and their antennas pointed skywards.

@ the Holy Water font the Spirit told him:

> You shall not go around slandering people!
> --Holy Gospel

Saw Elaine emerging from the Sacristy baring loaves & chalices for the communion.

Deacon Nina, & Elaine, verger, have provided me w/a food basket— mucho appreciated.

I am fairly sure or assuming—the only thing—when we feel it is fulfilled, this work, this mission of my life; then there will be no other things longing in my soul.

Forgive us our sins:

> Our sins we commit, knowingly
> Sins we do, unknowingly
> Sins done on our behalf

18

The Sermon spoke of the necessity of forgiveness: *Forgive your enemy and elevate yourself that way.*

The sermon drove him crazy; felt he should crawl back out the way he came, on all fours like a dog, over the circular labyrinth imbedded in the marble floor; out thru the massive iron Gilberti doors, down the Great Steps, down Taylor Street, home, shaking his head; *Oh God, Oh God forgive me God!*

Forgive your enemy elevate yourself in the eyes of God!

I am not broken—just tired.

TM Adventures In Pissing—202. Pissing in the park. (Referring to that incident while driving around w/Brother Baz, and me attempting to climb up a steep hill to find privy-cy behind a bush!

PM
Downton Abby a Brit TV serial depicts working women of the 19th century. Very little choice for a woman. In service—domestic to the rich, upstairs maid, downstairs maid; nanny—for only a more educated girl; or laundress. Very hard work, so little rewards. Then came the Industrial Revolution—many women left service and flocked into the factories for more money and greater independence—they could maintain a room and come and go as they pleased.

The former ruler of the Ukraine has slipped away in the night—packed a vehicle w/his bags, disappeared, & is now a wanted man! HA HA HA HA!!!!

The new interim appointed ruler declares the Ukraine must continue to move closer in the direction of the West, the European Alliance—and freedom, which is what the protesters demanded, what they gave their lives for!

Manhunt for former president of Ukraine—calling him a murderer of protesters. A warrant out for his arrest. Further, upon going into his private palace, and opening his affairs, see how much this thief has stolen, such wealth and opulence! Dozens and dozens of new expensive cars!

If a mother dies too soon, before she has a chance to imbue her young w/self confidence, a feeling of being protected; before they gain enough strength—you can expect the world will have to do the rest of the finishing up.

Monday, February 24
Am now @ Coyote—hear drift of unpleasant Hawk voice reading from memory what's preoccupied her mind—ages of female movies stars.

—Sun blazes bright. —

An anonymous blax girl sits smoking; am in her drift; had missed the primary table/chair by seconds—now subject to 2nd hand smoke.

Life grinds on & it is not always pleasant, but always bearable—thus far, thanx be to God. Weight is up—creeping up due to less testosterone, and to additional food—MOW.

Gather ye rosebuds while ye may.

ELLIS ACT FIGHT GOES TO SACRAMENTO!

(That is the State capitol.)

Good to know people are acting on my behalf.

That's what they earn a living & they make it life really graphic.

1849 church founded. The debate goes on!

Transmen. Oh this life is hard. Its hard for us God.

The Malaysian testifies to her ailments, and declares, almost happily, in a sardonic way: *good, maybe soon I'll make my exit.*

Doctor here, sitting here in the Ho's parking lot in his car— he's making a work call—*Use any prior anesthetics?* And all the etcetera of his career.

PM
Nada.

Sun blazing bright. However wind blows steadily. Reggae music played over loudspeakers.

So the OM sat in sun & breeze w/no one; entertaining dreams of fame & glory in his head & he coffeeed w/his now extant funds.

My Way is the only Way; says God.

The OM replied: *I agree, I agree.*

What makes the birds suddenly take off from sidewalk where they were milling about pecking for crumbs, and fly? Not a noise or gesture of a hostile dog or person; seems no reason @ all!

Maybe it is a sudden gust of wind, which catches them, to pull them up to the sky w/no effort of wing-flapping—where they swarm together in a centrifuge across the sky!

Birds scatter here & there in the wind. Sun shines. Everything is moving today not just sitting restive @ all.

Thank You God declared the OM, *for listening* to me.

The doorways exchange one homeless for another over short periods of time. Doorways built of stone—mortar, concrete—they last generations—until they are torn down to be modernized.

The lost go to sleep there, they have no where else.

> So yer' shivering! Wal' you din't bring a jacket like I instructed you!
> --Irish tourists in SF.

PM

21

Vatican. Expose:

Fraud
Pedophilia
Sexual assault
Personal advancement
Profiteering
Money laundering

TV Program about the Black Muslims—in America:

We are not like the white man who has built up cities from one end
of this nation to another, said he will use you, if you will not use
yourself.
--Honorable Elijah Mohammad, founder Nation Islam USA

There is one thread which can be extracted running thru all this—the
Vatican, w/its massive cover-ups of pedophile priests—abuses which
are accruing new, to this date—the lack of female priests –women
injected into the Vatican Men's Club to shake up the old boys only
business as usual; and the statement of Malcolm X:

The reason I left Nation of Islam can be summed up w/the
following, that the 80 year-old Elijah Mohammad is the father of 8
children, 6 of which by 6 different mothers, all girls under the age of
15.
--Paraphrased from Malcolm X

Black Muslims is a very hard line male dominated organization—no
questions asked.

Women's lack of power in some of the most powerful institutions on
earth—that which deal w/the spiritual.

Foreigners ask why blax been so lagging in finances and placement in
society.

Blax people in America is a story which hasn't played out.

There are still more chapters to go in the struggle for full emaciation
from the chains of slavery—and some of it is mental liberation.

To be white–& be, act like whites act was to adapt for sanity.

Documentary about the Black Muslims –began in Detroit w/a mysterious individual in the 1930's when racism was a suppressant to the black neighborhood, poverty was king. He was a lightskinned very handsome man who sold silk in the ghetto neighborhoods and taught the young Elijah Poole Arabic and the Holy Koran. Mysterious man was deported sometime later, and there he fades into history.

Elijah Mohammad held the Nation together 40 years; the underside of this was, among other allegations, 6 of his 8 children he fathered were by young teenage girls who worked as his secretaries.

Revelations of the extreme wealth amassed by the ruler of Ukraine— who has been dispossessed and is running to avoid justice—in a very short period of time he has acquired an estate so large it takes hours to walk across it. The palatial palace of the disgraced President is bigger in square acreage then the Vatican!

He left in a hurry—documents partially burned were found, but they did not have time to burn, so they were hurriedly snatched out of the fire and thrown into a lake.

The young victorious protesters have fished all these documents out of the lake and taken them to the National Library—they have all this equipment in the library—to dry out books, to preserve books as sometime accidents happen there; they spread them out to dry—fans turned on, blank papers, clean & dry stuck between the pages to aid the process, and one by one cameras snap images of their contents & post them online.

Thousands of documents of illegal transactions of the corrupt ruler are being broadcasted!

Am reading about Clementine Hunter, black folk artist—resident all her life of Louisiana, on an old plantation, lived to 101. Very prolific. Pipestem thin brown woman artist.

Another blax artist who creates wood sculptures using an ax to carve. I quote him: *An artist says I can't quit! I'm an artist! I got to keep producing!* His wife told him: *why don't you stop that and sit down and sell something!*

Once a very dear friend of mine told me the same thing—*why do you keep writing! Haven't you written enough?*

I was flabbergasted—then somewhat insulted!

Wednesday, February 26

White male yups, straights, are talking, @ Coyote.

> Create female offspring who have less vigorous seeds.
>
> New genetic codes.
>
> I'm saying genetic weakens begins in the genetic code much stronger version.

Seated @ Coyote, listen to latest plots, seditions, stories of the master race.

> Harness the genetic code. The genetic length.

But @ least they won't steal your backpack—the OM went to men's room—leaving all of his possessions safely on the counter top.

Power in the jungle plays.

Victory!

Winning @ the goal!

All my life I've been waiting for; well you know I have a job to do!

The OM paraded all the way back uphill from his Shrink.

Don't do anything some one else can do for you—concentrate on your work alone, your refined work.

24

PM

Well the latest hell worried about now is that my Bancroft check has not arrived. Must be here for my RENT due on the 3rd.

> Pussy. Just the word; made steam come out of her nostrils.
> --LUCY & MICKEY

Well the man in basement is back from the hospital and 2nd hand cigarette smoke has hit my unit again.

All this started years ago when the super greedy property management in conjunction w/the owner of this tenement added that basement unit—to make more money—and foolishly –unwittingly– moved a chain-smoker in downstairs.

Thursday, February 27

He had awoke that morning w/instructions from On High—that he was not to hate—but to neutralize all ill-will w/in his mind, somehow, and not hate. To not cause pain to any creature or being. On awaking further he recognized his own situation as a TS:

> A very violent & difficult life.
>
> Some of it if even just mental violence shown to us.
>
> And that when any regular person walks with us its important.

Every so often he'd cast up a pure prayer—not want anything in return. A prayer for a beast or person.

I had a game plan all my teenage years, & young adult—driving steadily forward into my 50's I had a game plan. Now I don't know where I'm going. I did my part of the game plan! But the world has responded very little.

Talked to Bonnie from the Bancroft—my check is on the wei! Also, they will pay out till near the end of June—then fiscal year begins. The check was approved—just not sent promptly since employees were off on January/February vacations.

Sky grey clouds darker like jagged jigsaw puzzle whose edges don't meet up perfectly; the bright blue sky & blazing yellow sun; a gold sun shine thru; it will rain.

Feet. The OM saw feet of passersby, as he sat in his café chair, scribbling.

Wait.

Do you think I Am the engineer of all things?

All faiths.

All faiths who believe in ME.

Bum shuffled by—clean white new tennis shoes from charity free box; the rest of him dirty, ragged; his face w/the ravages of abuse—you thrown you life away.

No—it was thrown away.

Talked to one of us who said he'd seen Cosmo w/2 pieces of his boy trade dining up the street—and this man added that privately he thought it is despicable.

I am wondering where all the old used up boys go? Don't see quite a few familiar faces around here any longer. —Well that's the despicable part.

Oh horror! The street is so clean! Its scary! Some yuppie territorial takeover? A Removal Of The Poor Plan set in motion!

The usual debris around trashcans, and thick in the gutters, discarded newspapers in tatters, coffee cups, the usual garbage been cleaned up!

Had a nice talk w/David Young V in Ho's parking lot:

> We never make any money being an artist. Never make back the hours of work—sell some work, it pays for my materials, and that's it. Never get rich, never have anything.

PM
> I see another stupid yuppie sto' gone out of biz — butcher-block
> paper pasted in the windows obscuring view of clean-up, move
> out—
> --CLOSER TO THE HOUR

Did I mention that stupid yuppie teeshirt shop finally relinquished its
hold—its brand name never caught on, its products barely sold, and
the kid who owned it could not sleep in the back room —effectively
using the space as store & live-in. He gone.

He is the tenant who complained his lack of customers was due to an
old tree out front which grew partially blocking the frontage view and
demanded it be cut down. I believe its branches were trimmed.

This entrepreneur had dreamed up a trendy brand name and was
trying to peddle his products, emphasizing its great name. Well
maybe he can sell the brand name for a small fortune to some bigger
outfit. People are profiting this way. The small fish allowing
themselves to be gobbled up by the big fish —for cash.

Friday, February 28
Am now @ Coyote, w/coffee. Thank you Jasmin.

She drove me to visit dentist—they fitted me up for a partial plate—
then she picked me up.

Told a friend over phone, who is struggling to get his top surgery paid
for by the state: *Its people like you & me we must keep on, we got to
push this thing thru—we just got to keep pushing it; just keep on!*

Later the doctor called him and said his surgery was scheduled for
Monday—so we have come a long way! A long way baby! — Since
15 years ago, when the state paid for nothing transsexual related—
including life-saving hysterectomy!

Yes new men, bleeding red blood, in pain, were denied services since
they were transitioning to men and the cruel overseers of the state &
private practice insurance alike claimed: *you brought it all on
yourselves!*

27

It's our birthright to be brought into perimeters of the gender we should have been.

Get work on teeth once again—all under the miniseries of Grace Cathedral—for I believe the state Senior Dental program has not yet started up—not until May.

Miss Lady …. Clatters past, fast, on tall boots. Filled up her leather jacket, cap, & nice slacks—she is riding high. She is riding high on the self-esteem of drugs—it takes this to repair the damaged psyche.

Blank winds sweep over the street @ a diagonal pitch—rain's coming.

He sat on another of his stations—his ledge.

We are all bundled up w/head scarves, coats, & shoes w/thick soles, wet backpacks & umbrellas. Rain approaches, OM going home.

Right now—hurry in, for rain is on its way!

—Oh spoke w/man in basement and it turns out it is the owner of the sushi restaurant who is smoking in the courtyard/basement, whose smoke is poisoning my air! He spoke w/sushi owner—& I haven't smelled smoke since.

PM
Nada.

Saturday, March 1
Homeless man sits on a Coyote chair scratching his head over & over & over, deep gouges w/dirty claw-fingernails; drug/ alcohol swollen fingers; wonders—*what happened to me?* Digs in his luxuriant hair—he is still on the younger side, but has an old man's grizzled face, bleary blue eyes.

Now picnic tables have been installed in the parklet—4 of them, their legs drilled down into the parklet floorboards, totally replacing the old metal table/chair arrangement—this will be far simpler for the help, no moving in/out—and hosing them down in the AM, according to owner. However my fear is they will attract homeless who will stretch out on them to sleep—one on each chair-bench, and one on top of the table—that's 3 multiplied by 4 tables—plus homeless attracted to this may camp out on the parklet floor between the tables—and they will leave refuse for the morning crew to clear away—but the owner says he doesn't mind if the homeless sleep out there (Middle Eastern man; does he have more empathy?) However the final problem will be, where homeless are, it attracts graffiti also, and the barista J, says they need to coat these fine picnic tables w/a coat of graffiti-proof paint—which allows the tagging to be erased easily as w/water—but how about all the rest of the café frontage? The suggestion would be to coat the entire café front & side w/graffiti resistant material!

This parklet sits in the street off the curb, taking the space of 4 parked cars sitting tail to nose—

So nice seeing Gary & we exchanged a hug. Got caught up briefly on each other's last business. I see how the new benches will work. Casual passerby's, oldsters must sit on the outside seat & not expend the effort to swing their legs up and over to the inside space.

Even young ones do this.

Now older blax gentleman who is a regular struggles to get into a bench. He adjusts the picnic table's parasol, so he is seated directly in its protection.

The homeless man sits in the rain, throws head back then bent forward into the rain.

A blax homeless goes past he stops bends down to speak to the bent-over homeless man, his head bends so low its pointing straight down @ the sidewalk red watch cap over his African hair; to get his face right down to see what the homeless white man is doing.

A once T-Girl dressed in a very proper male suit—looks handsome, but not herself; she didn't make the grade, and false church teaching told her God hates for her to try to become a woman—if she can live this way so be it. To try to live the other way—as a woman—was so painful because society did not see her as such—money for surgery, hormone treatments, trachea shave, (Adam's apple); beard removal— all so difficult the expense impossible for a poor person; society puts its religious dagger into our hearts; are we to be ourselves? Or to commit slow suicide? To die on the vine, longing, wishing for something we cannot be?

The blax bum has given the white young bum a full pristine cigarette—not previously smoked. It is an act of sharing.

Am waiting here, inside gazing out the plate glass window.

Can wait here an appropriate length of time, then on to the Ho's to procure my dinner.

New strength for weight-lifting night.

So—the kindly Operative @ Grace has provided me w/a partial plate & can resume dining fully. *You have been eating w/just your front teeth.* The dentist had said.

I want to see miracles!

Now he was mistaken about Godly thoughts again.

Maybe it was because it is approaching the Sabbath—in fact it is Shabbat! No the end of Shabbat! I am, (too apparently)—but nobody knows—talking about miracles like parting the red sea.

Saw an ex-member of Grace—in their 90's. Spoke about the ever-changing clergy, and the parishioners who drop away:

> I don't like the way they come & go—I think they don't care if we leave and go off to another church...
>
> They don't care because they don't stay themselves.

Buy one & get one free—howls a voice.

Loud drunken Academy students; gang of men & women, yelling.

HA HA HA HA!

He hit her ass so hard w/that bag of corn chips!

Exploded corn chips out of her ass!

A loud noise. One jock drops a carton of 24 bottles of beer—broken glass & beer foam scatter over the street.

That's why I wanted to carry it.

Later towards evening, OM and A. Ho, saw a black man entirely naked; showing his dark dangling junk, like an elephants trunk; of all things modern, he is talking on a cell phone —sat against the wall of a building—

I thought maybe he was wearing brown colored clothes.

Worn out clothes…

Thanks for an eye-opening experience!

So am not into the real thing so I might as well look @ it. Annie explains.

Middle-Eastern restaurant—Yemeni. Full of men! Find I dislike this—unless it's a gay bar! Because I feel it is part of the female subjugation, Middle Easterner's practice.

But fairly soon 2 female waitresses appear, one young, one old, and then young white female/male couples start coming in on dates.

Where are all the Middle Eastern women? Do they have any rights? Is their country, their culture, such a tyrannical regime?

PM
Nada.

Sunday, March 2

The Holy Water & lighting of the candle—the delta; the Crucifix; gentrification, the Sign of the Cross, the prayers. The prayers will be granted.

Grace.

My Grace I give unto you.

Some are broken. Some are struggling not to be broken.

All the OM could think was: *boy I'm lonely*—It was due to the reflective music; he felt he needed a sweet to cheer him—a coffee.

God's sheep waiting for the service to begin stood around the place here & there upon the marble circle of the great labyrinth.

Priest Mark leaving us; on way to Jerusalem. Shed the shining white garment of the configuration—and stood in a purple frock.

@ the service said our goodbyes.

Am in Pakistani restaurant w/Annie. Goat & spinach.

Everybody is uncertain—even the elders of the church.

View out of corner plate glass windows.

Nuke them—that's what the devils children do! They are angry! Want to react w/rage. Be like God.

PM
Did I tell you that 1 person has left us @ Grace and 6 more are in the process of leaving? My God! All of them fixtures around the cathedral since I've been attending!

Oh, Russia has invaded Ukraine.

Monday, March 3
The OM had finally arrived. He had arrived @ Coyote!

Spilled a portion of his café-o-latté—

32

Mad crazy folks talk about the Oscar awards.

The New Coyote—they succeeded in painting one of the picnic tables —but looks splendid—dark brown mahogany & hope they have sealed it properly. People are seated in it, young, put their feet in the right places which they have athletically achieved.

This athletic seating having been easily accomplished because they are young.

Well you got to get yourself, your affairs, all together for we never know what next will come upon us—people who don't are in despair.

Young kids, hop up out of their seats in the picnic tale agilely step on the bench w/gymshoed feet to get out—

One of us is back in hospital & must be housed by a caretaker until he recovers. The problem he can't pay 2 rents! So the state must step in and help him—to prevent him from becoming homeless when he recovers.

Benches are full of people now—most of the older ones sitting side-saddle on the edge—are chatting pleasantly. A human flock.

PM
Did I say? Internet is working—partially. This old computer might be the cause of it not being able to get everything clearly—like my Text POD. But can check on stuff! Am Connected!

Oh, in editing CLOSER TO THE HOUR #3—see I left a thread dangling—cat has been returned to owner downstairs—he checked himself into hospital, and had animal control come out and board his cat until his return—@ an affordable cost.

Tuesday, March 4
Well, we always have something that is killing us —& my weight is killing me.

I realize J's such a prima Donna; so upset & stressed out—maybe it is her high IQ—so now I am remembering what happened during our long relationship.

She is driving fast, fast w/one hand maneuvering complex twists in/out of traffic—while eating an apple!

Want nothing. Says the Lord/ess.

I pray for them; said the OM.

Especially for my own —& also for all the orphaned unwanted cats & dogs in pens.

Higher education. Whew! & I do mean Higher! (All my lessons, visions, illuminations @ Grace.)

Well am ensconced out here finally & thinking about things—that flit thru my mind; chiefly dealing w/street trade. While missing Olde's schooling. Glad I got to know that ROM while I had a chance—(Really Old Man.)

Due to the fact don't think he'll ever get back *up* on his feet—age 92, another stroke—I miss him.

Well the ex-owners flowerbeds are neglected where they're running to plain plants in the gold cauldron & no flowers. Greenery grows.

A white homeless in bright red hoody leans on one cauldron now—then he weaves out into the street into the slo-moving traffic—leans against a car only temporarily stopped @ the red light. Then he roils on—gravity taking him slowly downward, down these descending streets.

Oh, thought the OM—*my hands & fingers hurt.*

You no answering my phone call! You no answer my email! Spanish sister cussing out some no-good.

Now the gentleman was swinging one leg over the bench. Many people sit side-saddle—or straddle the bench one leg on one side, other leg on the other.

Men are pouring out of the mosque—Arabic conversations excitedly fill the air—the men head back to their chauffeur jobs in sleek cars w/ZZZ limonene plates; taxis.

Oh, by the by, that Rosetta stain glass window in the front of our Cathedral is called the Rose Window also called Canticle Of The Sun in Greece—which is in the city of Assisi St Francis is named after.

Many years ago someone wrote into newspaper why they went to church and saw these people acting so piously then see them later out in the street acting like thieves & dogs:

> The Church is not a museum for saints, it's a hospital for sinners.
> --Dear Abby

Up the uphill slant of Polk in front of the café, people walk home from work, carry a sack of grocery from the store—head bowed weary; world-weary.

PM
Well I see one of us has been sexually assaulted in a boy's toilet @ their highschool. An FTM. Thanx God/ess this young man has the courage to step up and file a complaint! To go public!

Jesus H. Flying Christ! TG teen falsified report of his attack in boy's bathroom in his High School! How embarrassing! However glad it is not true.

> He needs to keep looking a few moves ahead, as if it was a chess game.
> --Charlie Rose

After you're getting yourself too thru w/this world, a new one opens—

Reach.

Wednesday, March 5
Walking the long uphill back from Shrink.

Something is screeching high up on antenna upon a tall building; Van Ness Ave, uproariously screeching—it must be parrots. Green. A pair. They are fussing & feeding each other.

Gutted out building being tore down from it's top down; floors visible support columns, no-walls, scores of hallways open to the air & dust; bare door frames, story after story of ruin.

Jack Tar Hotel; then became Cathedral Hotel—now gone!

I was out early & it looked late—because sky was overcast totally.

Some people have to lie down & roll in their psychotic breaks.

It is a dark day. Overcast—sky thick, like cement encasing it, holding back, not a single rain drop let loose; forcing the sun back—so it does not shine on us, simply transits the heavens in oblivion and sinks to its rest un-witnessed, beyond horizon.

Junior rides off on his bike, green army coat like a cape furled w/wind, off to the store to spend OM's $2 on a strawberry milk.

He's back & looks good.

PM
Nada.

This is terrible, & will be confidential, will only say — Sista lady came over and said she had been feeling sad, so low, so her friend tried to cheer her up by braiding her hair—and this is the reason, —a year ago today her son was murdered; he was doing a good thing—driving somebody home into an unfamiliar neighborhood, people there didn't recognize his car & shot him. This is what's happening in our lower income neighborhoods.

Thursday, March 6
Am out @ Coyote—coffee—sun shines.

Feel God/ess is; sees me, feels me, —feel I am working for God.

Pigeons stalk about, red feet on flat wood slats of the picnic tables.

We are one human race connected—whither you like it or not you are going to deal w/society some way or another—if you want sex, its w/another human being; the food you eat has been prepared, handled, delivered, sold—by human beings; dug up out of the ground by human beings, discovered, invented by ancient humans—you can't get away from it! Then there is the old concept of the mountain men who drop out of society and go off & live in the deepest of wilderness for decades, alone w/no human interaction.

He sat there in the sun—yellow among grey, bright sky.

The mothers sat—w/fierce looks on their faces—defending their flocks while men were out doing all kinds of crazy things—going to war, climbing unnecessary mountains, searching for food among forests, gold among rocks…

Junior came by looking clean again, riding his nice expensive bike; he gave the OM a tuning fork—yes, that's right—a silver metal object which chimes a single note when struck—vibrating.

OM sat—very handsome young man sat nearby lips moving—is he out of his mind? Is he an actor memorizing lines in a script? An accomplished artist?

A homeless youth, —woe begotten— goes by holding his pants up w/one hand, which are dangerously slipping down over his narrow hips.

A different flock flew to him @ the Ho's; the OM tossed them crumbs.

Where was he going? What was he going to do w/his life?

The 8 pigeons looked well-kept—perfect red feet well formed—not yet stricken w/the gnarling disease. They were no doubt younger.

I see the afflictions before they begin.

Shiet! This world's such a mess & I'm still in it!

God let me be able to see your works—with my right eye!

Downstairs before the lecture started he questioned Annie Marie about the likelihood of food:

> Where's the potato chips?

> It's a Lenten lecture!

Well you get it—Lent means you are giving things up…

Compassion, empathy, & sympathy are all 3 different things—

So few people are taking courses in the humanities any more that educators have agreed—in their universities they are going to include Compassion in their technical, scientific courses—building it into the curriculum.

Building Compassion into the courses—most of us discover it on our own.

Animals—if someone is left behind in the pack, the senior member will go back & get them—

Neuro science—is there a genetic code, a neurological connection that creates cruelty and evil?

Psychopaths are a zero minus on the empathy scale. Super empaths are the saints—Mother Teresa, Desmond Tutu, and the like. One can be as low as a zero plus—these are the autistic people, the brain damaged.

You can teach empathy.

The Dean's lecture was excellent as expected.

Dean's owlish face peers down over the podium lectern in thick glasses and thick eyebrows.

Dean teaching ethical action.

Enlightenment in the Middle Ages—the idea of equality filtering up some men are all equal—not women, nor slaves— but soon the idea of female emancipation grew; and more men then before were included in this new equality.

1700rds the novel begins to arise as a major art form the humanitarian narrative.

1759 a philosopher wrote about acting in the world w/sympathy to another human being.

Empathy is a modern term, 19th century.

Difference empathy & sympathy. Sympathy is to identify w/another's feelings.

Embrace—sympathy

Encounter—empathy.

Education of the soul is a Christian training.

Praying the same things over & over is very important because it shapes up education of the soul.

Enables opening up a space to think beyond the ordinary.

PM
Dumpster divers in Paris, France—go to supermarkets 5AM when the day's unfit food is thrown out into garbage bins. —It is wholesome, clean, and can be used to feed human beings. Occasionally the grocery stores are so vile they pour bleach over the dumped food to prevent the divers from taking it. This is an abomination. The whole thing is a scandal—but the EU is promising to make radical changes in this food waste problem by 2015. Approximately one-third of all

supermarket food is thrown into waste bins because it doesn't meet the visual criteria the customers have, and none of them will buy it.

The parable of the prodigal daughter:

> There was a young girl who was wild, headstrong, & feckless — she came from a righteous family who loved her deeply. She went to her Mother Dear & Father and requested: *please give me the portion of my inheritance now — so I can enjoy it while I'm young, instead of later when I'm too old to do anything fun.* So, they gave her her share of the inheritance — dividing it among her other sisters & brothers & off the daughter went — straight to town, and thereupon became a hoochie momma.

> She wore her skirts short and dangling bangles on her earlobes and nose and lips; she got tattoos and piercings and sky-hi stiletto shoes and kept company w/gangstas and men of means. She spent her fortune on her salon in which she entertained w/lavish buffets all the lowlife of the town, thieves, boosters, common ho's and such.

> After some years of debauchery she found her fortune depleted — as was her own physical condition. Alas, she had depleted another currency — her young fresh-faced look. Now indeed she was a wore-out ho — a true hoochie momma. The rent was come due and no one left in her salon had any money @ all. In desperation she went to the town ho house and got a job there as a maid. She was forbidden to entertain men, and she had to clean each girl's room, plus all the common areas. For this she got a place to sleep — in the laundry room — and scraps of food off the plates from party times. One day she confronted herself & her condition and said: *self, what a fool you have been — you are up here sleeping in a laundry room, working from daybreak to nightfall and eating scraps of scrimp pate, lobster tails that those mean hos has eaten the actual shrimp. And you, self, w/a loving home to return to, and parents who deeply love you and they gots money & a full refrigerator too.*

> So off she went — back to her parent's house. Someone saw her at the bus stop — and word got back to her peeps. When mom & pops spied her coming down the block they let up a great roar of joy and soon the house was turned into a party house. —Now one of the other kids got mad, saying: *mom, pops, haven't I been an obedient child,*

40

and never strayed, and you ain't nevah got a party like this for me! And the parents replied:

You we have with us always, but there is a great rejoicing for the sheep who was lost but now found. Or something like that. And dey all lived happily ever after!

Friday, March 7
Was nice being awoken by Jasmin & Henry (dog) this AM, she brought 2 sacks clean laundry & vacuumed & mopped all floors—then on her wei. I left shortly after.

Well I have been broken & put back together—not entirely in the correct shape & this, several times.

The OM wrote his Infernal NOTES in a rugged stance @ his desk w/disabled computer & 1 disabled eye. He was ready to go out.

On way up street to the café he spotted someone he knew and they had a big laugh about one of the yuppie shops, which had gone out of biz:

> The young man had no business. Absolutely no business, but quite a few of his young friends came by & hung out there.
>
> I told him he'd have better luck paying the yearly fee and renting a stall down @ the Ferry Building, or Fisherman's Wharf—where the tourists go in droves, and he'd be selling teeshirts for $20 right & left. He said: *I won't lower my brand name!*
>
> Lower your brand name! What name? Nobody knows what your name is now!

When he left the shop they found he'd painted everything inside black—including the bathroom. The toilet was black, the sink was black even the faucets painted black. The walls floors & ceiling were black. In fact when you went in there you could hardly see because everything was black. There was no light! You know it takes about 3 or 4 coats of primer to cover over the black and try to paint any different color on it.

Alan Kaufman called as I stood in the Post Office mailing 2 Amazon books—STREET DREAMS, & DOING IT FOR THE MISTRESS: *I just got the proposal for the anthology—the Outlaw Bible of American Artists—New York!* Am pleased only this morning had been thinking how I need a jumpstart for people of the public to know about my fine arts—and begin to drive some art poster/print sales. Its like when Richard Kasak published 8 of my fine queer books out of New York in mass-market addition; that put my name on the literary map.

So maybe this is the chance, which will help jumpstart me, just like Richard Kasak did—in 1994.

Sits out in sun seeing angry faces people of the poor & mad, and people w/purposeful & mildly content look—of the normal, the successful, the privileged; walk by.

Pigeon came by.

@ Ho's the Malaysian's friend told a brief tale about some crazy old alcoholic white man w/white wild hair who was yelling, screaming, and the police came by and took away his beer can and poured it out, and some young yuppie women was watching and was furious—she wanted to see him in handcuffs and taken away too, she was highly displeased thinking he should be removed, and meanwhile all of us are thinking *she* should be removed—her and her kind w/all their money who are eating up us poor out of our housing.

Amazon books flying on their way!

Sun outside—promises of a beautiful summer.

The old gay gang here @ Coyote:

> Oh, look @ that man's big dick! Look @ it flapping away! He must not be wearing any underwear.

PM
Many will say this life was just so hard, but it could have been so much better—if only XX had loved me, etcetera…

The Underground—a beatnik joint where a few gays hang out—is closed because they couldn't pay the juice. This happens periodically. A lot of counter-culture businesses can barely pay their rent; can't pay off the cops so there is a raid. They're busted on some phony charge which is usually dropped by the judge next day. Unless they catch a minor; under 21 for boys, under 18 for girls, on the premises. A few patrons are taken away & locked in jail for suspicion of selling drugs, or suspicion of felony lesbianism. The place can't survive, and becomes a grey dismal boarded up door fronting on an alley off the avenue, a dingy hotel above it; gates folded across in accordion bars, where immediately passerby's start tossing refuse & newspapers & it becomes a garbage dump.

JOIN THE POLICE FORCE! A sign proclaims. TOP SALARY, TOP PROMOTION, SERVICE! And some street person has scrawled an addendum—'TOP PAYOFFS FROM PIMPS & LOTS OF GRAVY!"
--LUCY & MICKEY

Well I'm moving! @ a snails pace—I'm moving! Have resumed keying in L & M into disc for ebook; it is among my greater works—only 200 pages to go!

Saturday, March 8
Go out of house such raw terror see everywhere drugs—a crazed, furious blax man, unkempt suffering from insanity plus substance abuse howls down the street swinging a heavy sack @ people, things slamming it against café advertisement sandwich board.

WHAT YOU LOOKIN' AT! He screams.

Crashing past lurching, hitting everything w/flat surface in his path—a tall man & his woman date were walking his way arm & arm—they stop and turn around to walk back up the opposite way.

Polk Strassa is rough—better uphill.

People moving, carts & things, animals go past.

People, money; things. Always put people first. You can get love, friendship, companionship, from people… always put people first,

43

not things. But that's what some people do—they put things first always.

PM
I have spoken about the lost Malaysian plane—220 passengers, gone down in the South China Sea, it is believed. Suddenly went off radar; all messages stopped, and it vanished @ that point. And international crews of China, USA, Vietnam, Australia, Malaysia are all going in to search & rescue if possible—but nothing is to be seen—but a miles long oil slick commiserate w/jet fuel tanks, discovered by the Vietnamese yesterday.

Sunday, March 9
Humanity was not made for the Sabbath; the Sabbath was made for humanity.

Some take the holy day so seriously it becomes an impediment.

The 8th day this is thinking outside the box.

By this time the OM had done his rounds both starting from the left transept and from the right.

He bowed to the Cross. *Simple.* Says the Lord.

Prayed for his lame eye.

We want transformation without having to change.

The desert is —place of wrestling; place of contemplation, of stark beauty; place the early mystics went to do their contemplative meditation in monastic caves.

The road is so hard; and my burden is so heavy.

> *What wondrous love is this that caused the Lord of bliss to lay aside his crown for my soul, to lay aside his crown for my soul—for my soul.*

PM
Just heard from building manager:

44

Its those people who work for Google.

Tekkies.

Yeah, its them whose driven the rents up—they work down there in Silicon Valley, but they want to live up here—because they want to live in a city. They've grown up in a suburb all their lives, in a middleclass homes, now they work in a suburb; so they want to live in a city for the first time.

Ughhhhh.

So this makes it far worse, even more egregious—the selfish pigs—they are greedy. They have perfectly good houses— better made houses w/new faucets & toilets, & bug/rodent free walls, & spacious rooms w/up-to-date kitchens; down there in walking distance of where they work instead of gas guzzling miles & miles distant, but they chose to live all the way up here no matter what the price to the environment—us.

40 ships & 22 aircraft are searching for the vanished Malaysian plane.

Our universe is 13.8 billion years old.

Red Jordan Arobateau
Tuesday, April 8, 2014
2:45 AM, Pacific Standard Time
San Francisco, CA